PRIVACY

PRIVACY

JUSTIN QUINN

CARCANET

First published in 1999 by
Carcanet Press Limited
4th Floor, Conavon Court
12–16 Blackfriars Street
Manchester M3 5BQ

A CIP catalogue record for this book
is available from the British Library.
ISBN 1 85754 416 1

The publisher acknowledges financial assistance
from the Arts Council of England.

Set in Bembo by XL Publishing Services, Tiverton
Printed and bound in Great Britain by SRP Ltd, Exeter

FOR DAVID WHEATLEY

ACKNOWLEDGEMENTS

I would like to thank the following for their help and comments over the last few years: Brendan F. Dempsey, Robert Cremins, Selina Guinness, Aisling Maguire, Sinéad Morrissey, Michael Schmidt, and lastly, David Wheatley, to whom this book is dedicated.

Thanks are also due to the editors of the following publications in which some of the poems first appeared: *College Green, HU, The Irish Review, The Irish Times, Oxford Poetry, Poetry Ireland Review, PN Review, Poetry Review, Thumbscrew, Quadrant, Verse*. 'Insomnia' was published as a broadsheet in a limited edition of 250 copies by Bernard Stone at Turret Books (London, March 1997).

Grateful acknowledgement is made to Liveright Publishing Corporation for permission to reprint part of Hart Crane's *The Bridge*, and to Academia Publishers for the passage from Jan Patočka's *Kacířské eseje o filosofii dějin* (Prague, 1990).

CONTENTS

So, must we from the hawk's far stemming view,
Must we descend as worm's eye to construe
Our love of all we touch . . .

— HART CRANE, *The Bridge*

Na nejdůležitější modifikaci, kterou přinesly pozdější představy, upozornila H. Arendtová, když poukázala k tomu, že sféra domu nyní není jádrem světa vůbec, že je to pouze soukromá sféra, vedle níž vystoupila v Řecku a Řími jiná neméně důležitá a jí oponující sféra veřejnosti.

— JAN PATOČKA, *Kacířské eseje o filosofii dějin*

LANDSCAPE BY BUS

Look out the window – half
A landscape, half its trees.
Switch focus. Reflections of
The rest float by on these.

At sixty miles an hour
The world's being folded back
Into a suitcase. Where
Oh where will I unpack?

6.55 A. M.

5
Abseiling down
A rope that stretches from an Alpine height
For miles through rising temperatures to the small town
Tucked neatly in one corner of the valley floor
At such a speed, I have about
Five seconds left before
I brace and light;

4
While you're banking
With two advisers and the Premier
Above the city in the government jet, outflanking
Them with four minutes to go before you land
And they stride out to face the press
And make, as you have planned,
The country tremor;

3
While I'm going faster
Down a graph-curve about the anti-beef craze
And its effects on GNP (a clear disaster) . . .
Time equals T and three more units to the Crash
You were at pains to show the Premier –
One of the sheets you stash
Back in your briefcase;

2
And as events
Go swirling wildly out of order, you
Drive from the airport in your dusk-pink Italian Ventos
(Roadholding good on corniche and in wet conditions)
For two hours to the valley town
I'll land in in two seconds
Just as you come to

1
A braking halt,
With still time on the way to engineer
A last minute affair that is nobody's fault.
Now everything's happening so fast, the way we glance
And swerve by mountains, phalloi, parents,
The intervening distance
Approaching zer-

0.
Stopped dead,
Come skidding out of pastiche, out of text,
Into another that has us side by side in bed
With seven bells, we bathe here in a giga-watt
Of sunlight, dazed and twined together
And not sure as to what
Will happen next.

A STRAND OF HAIR

I never asked you for your hand,
Or in some man-to-man talk asked your father.
So light will be our wedding-band.

The other day I found an errant strand
Of your dark hair and held it, like a tether,
And though I never asked you for your hand,

We will be married, and
As this, hardly to be felt, twines round my finger,
So light will be our wedding-band.

So light that five years hence who could demand
Their freedom? From what, tied like this? Neither
Asked the other for their hand –

One London summer's morning it just happened.
The sun's rays wound gold heat about us there.
So light then was our wedding-band.

And you won't ask me to leave my rain-cursed land
Forever for your city with its saner weather.
I'll never ask you too. Give me your hand.
So light will be our wedding-band.

HÁJE

That's where we live. That's where the Metro loops
Back on itself and heads for town again.
That's where we step on escalating slopes
That draw us slowly up into the open
That's cleansed of trees; and massive concrete slabs,
Each studded with three hundred windows, icon
And estate, are simply everywhere.
A Marlboro billboard reminds me about nature.

That's where the city, driving southwards, ends
It's true (a smaller group of towerblocks noosed
By nothing, forest, wasteland where the highway bends
With freedom into open space, unloosed
At last and breaking from the city's bounds,
Nosedives for Wien), but nothing is released
Where nothing starts and stretches well-surveyed
To the horizon, toward which pylons stride and fade.

APARTMENT

You're drawn up to a tree's height in the air.
You leave the lift, unbolt the bolted door
And slam it shut behind you, home once more.
Relief. Unzip. Undress. Run the shower,

Unopened mail left waiting on the shelf.
Water scalds your body, steaming open
Your every pore, limbs slide around the soap in-
Side the tub. Step out and dry yourself.

Looking out the window, you see the forest,
Its black bar, the still-light sky and left
Of this another block, another lift,
Another hundred lives that felt the frost

In the fifteen minutes from the Metro home,
And lean back with a drink into the chair.
You watch one woman and then become aware
She's stopped her rhythmic strokes, put down her comb

And sees you. One instant and you have exchanged
It all. And nothing, when you twist the blinds
And turn back to your book that maybe binds
Huge things together, has everything arranged

From nations to the Derridean trace,
Voluted columns after columns of prose
That put things in perspective, balance praise
With scorn to hold the pantheon's roof in place.

It suddenly shivers like the trompe l'oeil
It maybe is beside the recent vision
Of a woman home from work, her earned seclusion,
So like you that you wonder if some play

Of light threw your reflection back into
Your drowsy eyes or you back into hers.
The moment of mirage and truth occurs
In the apartment buildings' interview,

A different kind of world from what you read,
A different kind of life from what you had
For years in that old house beneath the Hrad.
You find yourself inside this block of concrete

That's setting fast, like everybody else
Halfway to being bar-graphs, stacked in boxes
Across the south-town's *locus*
Un*amœnus* and dog-shit-covered green-belts.

And look at these, what's more, these ringing blocks
Laid down upon the whiteness of the page.
They try to draw you into their stiff cage.
(Whose wires are far too wide. Which no key locks.)

'Yes, and . . . ?' Well, life, as Joseph Cornell knew,
Is always an affair of different boxes.
Take these ones. Be my guest. What this place lacks is
Chaos. Impulse. Colour. Over to you.

BATHROOM

With cans of paint, some brushes and the radio
You disappeared today into the bathroom.
Incensed by its pure whiteness – enamelled rime
Of tiles and chalk-rough walls, their blinding ratio –

You came home yesterday with special paints
That hold their own on even those white surfaces'
Gloss and glare, and would metamorphose
Where we wash teeth, comb hair, keep stuff for pains

Into long panel after panel of blue
And yellow and green; a flower inside each one
Inside a room with no way in for sun –
A fight between the gridded immovables

And something that will always hate right angles
And smashes them to pieces when it wants,
But ends here in a startling détente
Of shapes and colours, just the few odd wrankles

Where brushstrokes overtake the tiling's bor-
Ders. All of which you kept a secret, locked
For hours in there. The only news that leaked
Was what the radio murmured under the door.

Swung open at long last as you mildly storm
Into the room to tell me it's on view,
Your hands still dripping yellows, greens and blues,
And touch me, colours flaring to my arm.

SIX HOUSEHOLD APPLIANCES

1   HOOVER

It picks up mainly pieces of us,
Small flakes of skin, odd hairs, an eyelash,
Then paperclips and grains of food
Gone hard where they fell three weeks past.

Every so often it's fit to burst
And there's this touching scene: the bag,
Split sometimes down the middle, is lifted
From the plastic vacuum chamber
And you can see it all conjoined
In wadded bliss at last: us there
With everything we sidelined, edged
Off tables, worktops, chairs and shelves
While forging our lives on ahead.

Dumped in the bin. The bag replaced.
And I'm off roaming round the flat
Again with this huge hungry wheeze,
This loud dog on a leash, resolved
To clean up, get our lives in order.

2   ICEBOX

How did a block of winter
End up inside this flat
Of creaking radiator,
Of nuclear-station heat,
This tropic where with languor
Palmettoes yawn and spread?

Ask rather how a towerblock
Of hottest summer stands
Oblivious to the bleak
Cold without. It astounds
To think about the deadlock
Temperatures and stunts

That winter pulls with snow
(The landscape overnight
Erased); how even so
We still survive inside
This cosy hell, how you
Will often walk bikini'd

While frost exfoliates
Across the window-pane.
Today, the radio states,
It could reach -13.
The icebox imitates
This chillingly alone.

It stores the sun for us –
For instance rock-hard blocks
Of vegetables, still fresh,
Whose complex photosynthetics
That once drew sunlight, freeze,
Put by as winter stocks.

Here too our spirits reside.
The vodka bottle frosted
While (contradiction stowed
In contradiction) the lustrous
Fluid moves inside.
It pours out, calm, unflustered,

Into the glass, itself
A glassy syrup. We've learnt
In deep December to slough
Off everything that's barren
With this small water. When quaffed
We feel its ice-cold burn.

Despite its tight corset
It stands full-bodied on the searing hob
With one black arm akimbo. Of course it
Seethes the whole while long, since that's its job,

But otherwise stands firm.
The little Java surging to its crown
Does not erupt beyond its form
And make a Pompeii of the flat and town;

I have to say I'm grateful.
As well as for the thimblefuls of tar
That take god knows how many cratefuls
Of coffee bean to make, and months to mature.

The grounds sit in their chamber
While underneath the water churns in turmoil
Until the pressure and the temper-
Ature get to it and a gathering thermal

Lifts it into flight.
It showers up through the perforated floor
And infiltrates the cell outright.
The least and last ground is cleansed of all flavour.

Then filtered by the moke
It bubbles up the home straight – huff and puff.
See how the aperture gives a choke
And gushes forth the pure, the dark brown stuff.

Which is all very well
Until you clean the tiny cauldrons out
And prize apart the clam-tight shell
Inside of which the grounds adhese like grout:

It's such a mess to wash.
The attitudes in which they came to grief –
Sucked clean of essence by the whoosh
Of my need for refreshment and relief –

Those terror-stricken forms
Crumble like shale as the water takes its toll.
Across the sink they sweep enormous
Estuaries . . . then vanish down the plughole.

4   NUCLEAR REACTOR

Although it's rigged up in the middle
Of nowhere, it's our new cathedral,
Dead centre of a complex model
Of lines and cables, where polyhedral
Chains break down, the national griddle

That fries up isotopes for power.
The squabbles and the overreactions
That keep occurring hour after hour
With catalytic provocations
Inside the private chamber shower

Their energetic favours on
The land at large: for instance, cities,
Curved wide across the wide horizon,
Set midnight skies ablaze with these;
For instance, all the television

Unfolds with light in front of us
Is powered by these explosions; for instance,
Streetcars taking corners, office-
Buildings live with shares and options,
The hoover making handy refuse

Of our apartment clothed in dust –
Illuminations, metamorphoses
That arc through our all lives – induced,
You'll find if you sing back through fuses,
Wiring, against the electronic thrust,

If you go singing back and back
Through ten transformer stations, the grand
Systemic web that serves our lack,
All's brought to life by that hard grind
Of atoms underneath the stack.

Which leaves us at square one again.
The scope within that crucible!
How many times outstripping Röntgen's
These rays rebound and surge, unable
To break out, like tightly shackled dragons

Who if they find one crack will blow
The lot sky high; and then arise
And sweep through open cloudlands, billow,
Breathe, unfurl. And then erase
Everything their shadows touch below.

5   KETTLE

In Central Europe I placed a kettle on a hob
And waited in the kitchen. And from its watery depths,
From deep down at the element itself, the sound
Of North Atlantic surf came crashing storming out.

6   WASHING MACHINE

The dirty clothes
Have mounted up the whole week long
Inside the wicker basket:
Sudariums on which our loves and salts
Have left impressions – strong,
But getting rid of them won't blow a gasket.
Throw in the powder and start the waltz
Of clothes round clothes

Round clothes. Look in
And see the sudded galaxies
Of underwear and T-shirts,
Of jeans, of everything that makes us decent;
See how it all relaxes,
Like it doesn't give a damn and just reverts
To primal goulash, life unreasoned;
All this locked in

Until the drum
Comes whirling to a stop. Clean vapours
Fog the glass door-plate.
My hands reach deep inside and gather up
The mass of sodden fibres
That's like a soul, a dull amalgamate
Of our appearances, a pulp
Of styles so humdrum

You'd never think
That this is what we use to show
Our chic selves to the world.
The clothes must be dried out, ironed clean of crease
Before we'll let them go
About us – cuffs buttoned fast, belts tied, scarves furled –
And all our great civilities
Regained, we think.

The appliance dreams
Our habits through the nights and days:
Roused when drugged and blear,
Sent out into the world, brought back, a laugh,
Some film the machine replays,
Then spinned to sleep. That we assume we steer
Our lives is yet another of
Its programmed dreams.

SILENCE

November, and the sluggish orbits of a fly
Around the room are driving me insane.
It rests a second on the window pane
And my book flattens it against the sky.

That instant a truck outside starts grunting from its bonnet.
Give me a mountain range to swing down on it.
Give me a deadly viral strain that quells
The pounding of all next-door neighbours' blood cells.

SPYHOLE

My eyeball grooved into this hemisphere,
This stud of solid glass, I see the world
Beyond the door of our apartment swirled
Into strange shapes, as unreal as they're clear:

The white-walled corridor, fluorescent lights,
The other doors that wait there for an opening,
All comically bent round my eye, all sloping
Under duress in the lens's sights.

I lift my head away and suddenly
Things have the look of truth again: the chairs
Don't curl around my gaze, the table bears
Its load of fruit and papers steadily,

The walls keep floor from ceiling, perfectly flat
And upright. Unlike the curved grotesquerie
Kept safely outside under lock and key,
This is real. This is where we're at.

Or rather, I am, at the moment. You're
Beneath the city on the Metro home,
Making the transfers, straphanging to the hum
And racket of each subterranean contour.

I shadow you the last stretch, leaving the wagon,
Then up and past the upright ticket stocks
Into the night, between the dreaming towerblocks
To where you reach home and are real again.

INSOMNIA

We lie at night,
Blinds flush against
Streetlights burning
Five floors below.

We lie because
I sleep, you don't:
Statements of love,
We two are one,

Etc., these
Faded quickly
When I was dragged
By dark hands down

And out to where
A Buñuel film
Of my childhood
Is the feature.

I'm swimming through
Myself as through
A kind of dark
Marvellous honey.

Streetlights still burn
Your retinæ.
And you begin
To turn on me

Purely because
I sleep, you don't.
And toss, and burn,
And twist, and yearn

To be erased,
Your mind wiped clean
Of everything
It's ever known.

But not a chance.
Obstinately
And humming loud
As hell it goes

And goes and goes.
(He sleeps, I don't.
He sleeps, I don't.)
Then it doesn't

An hour or so.
And this is how
We lie at night,
Streetlights burning.

CHILDISHNESS

Dream-father, wind
Sweeps in across the forest, through the streets,
A ghost that howls its wound
Through every keyhole that it meets.

Dream-father, here
We have been cornered, in this apartment-block,
With its scream climbing higher,
Its plans to undo brick from brick,

Head over heels,
To smash us through the fields, across the highway,
Littered to the hills,
Our selves scaped out beneath the sky.

DREAM-FATHER: Wind,
It's only wind, which these shapes can withhold.
I know, for once I wound
Them tight about myself, my lovers, my world –

I've since untied,
And watched their continental-drift apart,
Salts of the earth that died,
But not before being loved, being part.

★

Up on the fifth floor
Of this benighted building, we lie in bed
And listen to rain scour
The windows angrily with beads.

We could doze off
And sleep through the storm's gathering furore –
Rain-punishments, explosive
Thunder, ray after cancer ray

Of nuclear wind –
And wake to find the city mobilised
In cars and buses, twinned
With somewhere on TV, policed

By foreign newsmen
Clambering for the best disaster shot.
And where would we be then,
Unhoused, unversed in that new plot,

Where everything
We know is wrong, no life left undenied,
No leg or stone left standing?
Why then, dream-father, then we'd need

The smallest hands
To heft our half-dead weight out of the old,
Work through the binding strands
And deliver us into the world.

Our childishness
Is such that it would take a child's small arms
To lift us up, judicious
Of our danger, and carry us from harm.

OR: we could fall
Asleep and wake to find the sunrise, a week
Of work ahead and all
Unmobilised, the storm a freak.

In which case we,
Dream-father, will do the same for it and slap
It wide awake. Rest easy.
Here's the morning. Now, *you* sleep.

HIGHLIGHTS

Last night the couple in the flat above us
Were in full flight: tirades and injured feelings
Swung back and forth for hours across the ceiling
Like bad jazz solos, long and repetitious.
Last week we caught crescendos from Sibelius.
And now tonight around eleven stealing
Through carpets and concrete slabs a wild, freewheeling
Moan of utter joy, which is their Anschluss.

But otherwise we'd never know they're there
And easily forget their sixth-floor sitcom.
We get on with our own lives – work and leisure,
Chores tending to our household appliances –
Which seem the same as theirs (the noise, the rhythm)
Apart from what goes on between, in silence.

NEW APARTMENT:
TERENURE, 1968

Stacked and scattered here and there
About the main room of the flat
The boxes, chairs and bulging suitcases
Have skidded to a sudden standstill.
My parents start arranging things.
They bring the table to the kitchen,
Considering its shape and size
Against the kitchen's for a minute,
Then place one edge against the wall.
They unstrangle lamps of their flexes.
They try to imagine their future life
With the new couch there, or there,
As though the choice that they make now
Will set them on one course for years.

The TV is a square of solid shadow
Securely housed in imitation teak.

Switched on. A phosphorescence starts to speak.
They watch the country turning through a talk-show.

The country stretches to the rocks
And sand and cliffs and promenades
Which mark the island's end; the fields
And hills and that one rainy street
Through which the border runs; standing
Idly by itself in mohair,
With patriotic decency.
The floor space of their new apartment
Makes up one tiny tract of this.

Free of their parents' furniture and prints
They love to plan and switch and rearrange.

Things brim with possibility, with change.
Themselves in three months to become new parents.

For six or seven days they labour
To make the cosmos I'll inhabit.
I orbit in my mother's stomach
Oblivious to the fact that soon
I will be made to move as well.

THE MOVING HOUSE

for Shane and David

I'm thirteen. We're in a car
That westers with a caravan in tow.
Nobody's speaking in my nuclear
Family just now entering Mayo.
Transported miles from home, round lakes,
Up into clouds by virtue
Of the winding mountain-route the trunk road takes,
Past fields and valleys, the odd fine view
For which we stop, religiously
Alight, are told to 'take that in'
(Both the parents sigh),
And then are stuffed into the car again,
The road resumed, the hedgerows and the fields
Along the roadside blurring by,
Us slumping back into the seats,
We're on our holiday.

★

No, it began, in fairness,
Once the caravan was parked and jacked down fast,
When we would start right off to furnish
It with all the stuff devised
To make our home from home, well, civil.
Everything from the mat,
The teacups, clothesline, **Swingball**™, shovel,
To, dazed by this strange move, our mutt.
We thought it was hilarious,
His nervous scampering everywhere
To mark the place with piss,
The way he checked it and rechecked it, unclear
As to how the house could put on wheels and move
Into a field (hmm, have a scratch)
By sea and mountains. Of course, he'd have
To keep a careful watch.

★

Saucepans on the verge
Of taking flight occasionally – destination:
Somebody's deserving head. A surge
Of rage, they're ready for lift-off; Shane
Or David or I seethes on the brink
Of obtaining satisfaction.
But you could never get a decent swing
Inside that pokey caravan
So you'd settle for a maul instead.
'All hell is breaking loose in here,'
My mother'd shout to get
Jack in to break us up. A clump of hair
Grasped tight in each of the combatants hands,
We'd stand there fuming for a while,
Then skulk back to our corners, hemmed
By those four fibre walls.

Some nights were just for parents:
Jack and Anna would drive off for a meal
To Stella Maris or The Lawrence,
Investing me as viceroy of their weal,
While even then the plebs conspired
To overthrow my rule.
The traitors, Shane and David, when caught, were spared
The blade – I was merciful.
But my benign dictatorship
Fell just as soon as we copped on
That daylight things like sheep
And bushes were now ghouls that could creep in,
That everything for miles about us there
Would stay sunk in that utter darkness
Till morning; and we realised the horror
Of a world without our parents.

Mornings. Waking up
And stumbling half asleep out through the door
Into that unroofed space, the hoop
Of the horizon stretched miles clear
Out to the sea's expanse, then tucked
In at the hills behind –
The huge Atlantic sky, its windlines tracked
From swooping waves to solid ground
By clouds that idle their slow way
With solemn elemental ease.
How should one spend a day
In view of revelations such as this?
What occupation, game or bright career
Is worth a damn beneath striated
Skies like these, but watching, here,
Their passing overhead?

Lone gazers had their day
For about five minutes, till everyone was up
And stowing sheets and bunks away.
Who's first to wash? And where's the soap?
The breakfast things are clattered out
And we sit down together.
Everyone's hair looks weird. We start to eat.
Seeing David taking all the butter,
Shane roars and soon the five of us
Join voices with the choral parts
That took long years of practice,
Tears, to get down to this pitched fine art.
A sudden coda's reached with two curt smacks
And we silently resume our breakfast.
Outside we hear the mocking cackles
Of gulls disputing crusts.

War! The fields and dunes
Turn into glacis, forts and no-man's land
And we're now rebels and dragoons
As the Irish take their glorious stand
Against the English. But who'll play *them*?
Finally, despite his red hair,
Shane says he'll lead the King's men – which means him,
The dog, a brush and nothing more.
We start in earnest. David and I
Should win but somehow we end up cornered
And out of ammo. We try
For the caravan to keep ourselves covered.
History demands he burn us out
And shoot us. But he knows it's wrong
And loses heart. Soon he's routed
And we sing our soldiers' song.

If I'd looked out one day
I might have seen a car up on the ridge –
Some people looking out its window
Intently at the field. They reach
A standstill and the doors swing open.
One of them is me
Fifteen or so years on, the next a woman
I married one month previously.
He turns to tell her something: sham,
Because he points a good bit off
From where I actually am.
His stories too are probably just the stuff
To get them both nostalgic, tinted rose,
Poetic truths not facts. They stare,
Get in again and as the doors close
Fade back into the future.

GREETING

for Selina Guinness

We'd just be swinging round on Pearse Street into work
When I'd look up occasionally and see your window:
The wildest coloured cloths hung out and waved in answer.

PODZIMNÍ KUPLET

The trees have hoarded sunlight all year long.
The order comes in autumn: release it.

WEEKEND AWAY

This long weekend we're here in an apartment
Right in the centre, off St Stephen's Green,
Ten minutes walk from everything to clubs,
Museums, buskers, chain-stores, cinemas
And bars. The place was offered us by friends
Off west to Galway, to leave it all behind,
Their all to serve us as a hide-away.

Mornings have the seagulls wailing torment
Through empty weekend skies; they swoop, so keen
To see deep shoals. Their arcs have chimney hubs.
A mile below them, awake and in amaze,
We have put to sea, are lifted high on fronds
Of waves, smashed downward, are lastly brined
And washed up on the bed beneath the duvet.

Beside us stands the Irish Permanent
Head office holding hordes behind a sheen
Of metal, glass and Brobdingnagian Chubbs –
The hoards of those who have, who can amass
Enough to build a home. But no ground rents
Are paid at night by the hundreds that we find
Stretched out on pavements for a cider soirée.

A landscape on the wall to ornament
The living room. A Connemara scene
Of bohreen, field and pole. Some fuchsia shrubs.
Black hills. Dark twilight. But something's gone amiss –
The twilight spreads beyond the frame, the fence,
Into the room and out beyond the blinds
Across the Dublin sky, across to Galway.

We hover in our spaceship, self-important,
Two floors above the brawls and shouts that mean
The bars have shut: *Up Ireland! Up the Dubs!*
Which fade towards two. We are anonymous,
Untouchable, looking on the street that wends
To Leeson's. Not a mugger stirs. And mind,
If he did, we'd lift off for the Milky Way.

With coffee and a bar of peppermint
You stretch out with your novel, the TV screen
Abandoned for Heathcliff running through the scrubs
Across the moors, his raging animus.
Another world inside these walls, which ends
And you drift all the long way back. Now bind
Your arms round me, your more real moorings, OK?

A different strand of hair is like a portent,
Licked round the inside of an otherwise clean
White oven dish (another in the tub's
Small plughole grille), a sign perhaps that someone's
Life, somebody else's life, will cleanse
This whole apartment space of us, in kind.
We buy a paper for each numbered day.

OFFSHORE

'I'm jumping. Relax a second.'
I pause then swing my arms.
Next thing my body's wakened
Like with fifteen fire alarms.
It's colder than I reckoned,

Like being thrown into acid
The first two minutes, then slowly
The stinging stops as it
Adopts my body wholly
To its depths . . . this morning placid.

I'm treading water. Colm
Is standing on the rock
About to dive. I call him
Names such as YOU CHICK-
EN, CHICK – he jumps and falls – EN.

We swim a good bit out
Then scull around to look
Back shorewards. Hereabouts
The cliffs rise gently, rock
On hulking rock, redoubts

That glitter with a million
Specks of scattered mica.
From here the path we filed down
Through those cliffs is like a
Stairway skywards. A mile on

Or so Killiney bay
Curves off from this rough spur
And ends up out at Bray.
The headland there's a blur –
The usual algebra

Of distance and perspective
Confounded by light mist
And the lack of our corrective
Lenses. But we're still amazed
By everything since our dive

Into this other world –
The light, the land and sky,
These rocks and stunning cold,
The brimming sea, chin-high,
Its glimmer. Us upheld.

RIVER SWIM

Well it pulls you shorewards just to swerve
You out into the mainstream once again.
You feel its suck and need about your body
Dangling from the surface into brown depths
Like clothes hung out on clotheslines. Its need is mountains',
How they're relieved to rid themselves of water,
Raindrop meeting raindrop in the thousands
Till numbers swell enough to make a river
Twisting through the fields the way a streetcar
Twists through towns, the speed, the force.
                                    You swim
With it. You glide by trees, a house, some people
For whom you're just a head the current takes
Wherever it wants. Indeed, you'd be a fool
To swim against its sense. This is the way
That mountains talk to seas a thousand miles
Or more away. Your best bet is to jump
Out at some easy point along the bank
Because in winter it stops dead, is ice.

EXAMINATION OF THE HERO THROUGH WAR AND COMMUNISM

Born 1904
in Moravia.
Farming family.
He left to study
medicine in Prague.
Launched his career
around the same time
as the country – called
Czechoslovakia –
and he rose with it
in learning, money,
acclaim in his work,
marrying a girl
from Prague. Settled down.
Was completely straight
in all his dealings
and as well as this
a gifted surgeon.
And then the Nazis.
Worse still, when they'd left
the Marxist buffoons
arrived in tractors
staying forty years.
Who hated his kind –
a compliment he
refused to return
with equal fervour,
considering them
more like an illness
that must run its course.
Besides which he had
two growing daughters

and queues of patients
waiting to be seen.
One of which daughters
became your mother.
You sit there often
with him at his desk
and listen as he
talks about the past
(family stories,
anecdotes; also
Edvard Beneš
ranting in a square)
which flowed through him, is
flowing strongly still
into the future.
You're carried with it.
But he, pulled by the
thought of parents,
grandparents, great- and
all the greater, now
turns and heads into
that current, swimming
so effortlessly
backwards against its
wide and twisting force.

DAYS OF 1913

The sun goes down on courthouse and mainstreet.
The grocer has his borsch and says as often,
'This soup the emperor himself could eat.'

His wife beams like a child given a treat.
They go to bed, wake up, but soon, again,
The sun goes down on courthouse and mainstreet.

Elsewhere, worked up into a righteous heat,
The postman thinks that scheming Jews will poison
The soup the emperor himself will eat;

While Beggar Breadhead sees the worthies meet
Out at the town's small brothel, but only when
The sun goes down on courthouse and mainstreet.

And war will sweep all this away complete –
No soup left for the grocer's meal, and even
No soup the emperor himself could eat.

All turned into nostalgia. Their words repeat
With longing in their children's children's children,
The sun gone down on courthouse and mainstreet.
'This soup the emperor himself could eat.'

from DALIMIL'S CHRONICLE

after the early fourteenth-century Czech

There is in the Serb tongue
A land whose name is Croats.
A chieftain once lived there
Who had the name of Czech.
He struck a free-man dead
For which he was accused.
This Czech had brothers six
Who brought him power and honour,
And so had many chattels.
One night he gathered them
And with them left this land,
The land whose name is Croats.
They went from wood to wood,
Through brakes and over mountains,
Their children on their shoulders,
Until at last they reached
A forest, dark and deep.
His people longed for home.
Czech said,
         – My deed be damned
That brought you to this strait,
Thick, tangled brakes become
Your only home and bed.
And Czech said to his men,
 – Let us go to this hill
And set the children down
So they may sleep. And try
To let our longing go.

At sunrise with his brothers
Czech stood upon the hill
Prospecting all that land.

Czech said,
                    – We go no further.
Here is the land we wished for.
Here we will have full trestles.
Here there is game and birds
And fish and bees enough.
Here we are safe from foes.
They saw this from the hill
And so they called it Říp.

To start, they had no bread
So they ate meat and fish.
The first year they dug fields,
The second ploughed them up.
And since their chief was Czech
They called the new land Czechs.

EPIC FRAGMENT

Then in the middle of it all
   I woke to find myself in a deep forest,
     The light dismal,
Moon-glow seeping downwards through the trees, and frost
   Enamelling the ground. That I could see,
     There wasn't any exit or pathway forced
Through the thick undergrowth to safety.
   I was shivering with the cold.
     I pulled my jacket tight about me
And started moving out, collid-
   ing now and then with trunks of trees and rocks
     Looming at strange angles from the earth – massive, solid –
Each time a shock,
   The shape impacting on me out of nowhere,
     Leaving me for moments dazed and shaken.
Far above, the sway and stir
   Of tree-tops in the wind. And even that was different,
     The slightest bit off-key: not a freshening air
That swept with a susurrus through the leaves, more like a front
   Of textured static, rippling
     Across the forest's ceiling. I turned back to the ground
And couldn't help but feel there was a hurried stippling
   In what I saw around me, as though it were rushing back
     From somewhere it had waited in reserve – bushes, branches,
                        trunks all grappling
Their way back into being once again, along the track
   Of my returning gaze.
     I couldn't focus and my head went slack.
I would have drifted back to sleep, but that I heard a shouted phrase
   In an earlier language; it was an order.
     Another voice, desperate, screaming begging please.
My breath came shorter.
   I moved in their direction, planting every step

As silently and slowly as I could, further, further...
As on a PA system there was a flow and ebb
    To the voices, as though they volleyed in and out of the past,
        And I couldn't follow all they said – something about *chattel*,
                                    more about *putting a stop*
To something, and no the other voice said no; then a revolver blast.
    I saw the flash like lightning through the trees
        Illumining the scene: a man there on his knees slumping down
                                    like ballast,
Two others standing over him, as if caught in a frieze.
    A moral tableau or glorious founding myth
        Or just the dirty work of thieves,
I couldn't tell. Then they were coming for me with
    Guns in their hands, as though preset (how else could they have known
        Exactly where I was?). Each chest a brickhouse width
Cased in a cuirass, arms braced, greaves fixed on,
    Fierce phosphorescent eyes blazing from the shakos.
        My moan
Of abject fear just made them quicken their pace. I could see the
                                    individual shackles
    That held the suits of armour fast, yet supple.
        And the shock was
How they had no real substance: they were a subtle
    Matrix of CAD graphics, not flesh and blood.
        Which wasn't to say they didn't mean trouble.
As with a joystick, my gaze was piloted
    To where a outsized weapon
        Lay nearby in the mud.
I picked it up and turned it slowly on
    The sprinting holograms.
        This was no normal gun:
Streams of nuclear-fissioned lightning flew like pogroms
    From the barrel,
        And, obedient to their programs,
The two exploded in a million pieces, going up with boreal
    Exuberance; turning, as they fell, into more points.
        Such was their burial.
By this time it was getting light: a bright expanse
    Was visible beyond trees and I walked toward it
        And found myself on a hill looking at the sun's advance
Up through a marvellous sky that must have hoarded
    Those wild colours for an age before releasing them.
        Spread out under it
Were towerblocks, at a standstill. It was around 7 a.m.

49

CINEMA

We were coming out of the local cinema yesterday evening after seeing the latest subtitled schlock from Schwarzenegger when a wave of homesickness swept over me. As we moved beneath the grimy pergolas of the mall, I was slowly abseiling down through the atmospheres through which I had orbited for two hours with the help of all those clever F/X people, to crashland back here again. The story was about the founding of some nation of rebels in a galaxy far, far away: their murderous but responsible leader, the hardship of their wanderings through space, etc. Earlier, ensconced within the black walls of the cinema, floating through its dark space, without really thinking about it I had felt that D— was waiting for me outside. Instead, this: people milling round everywhere, going in and out of the nearby Metro station, shouting, running, walking, speaking Z—. During the few seconds it took for me to adjust to the language again, it seemed almost comical that people were pretending to communicate through this gibberish. How could it convey real thoughts, insults, feelings of affection through the night air from someone's mouth to another person's ear? It was a joke. They didn't seem like people at all, just puppets stuffed out with the presumption that their emotions and ideas have the same substantiality as those of an English speaker. But as K. and I switched back into Z— I remembered that that's exactly how they see me, struggling with their unwieldy grammar and bevy of un-pronounceable words. I thought of the definitive Z— Grammar in which the crystal core of the language is laid down clearly. Because of the small size of the country, the rules governing spelling and usage in the Z— language can be set and controlled much more effectively than they can in English.

We had now come out of the mall and were crossing the road. Facing us were tens of large towerblocks all of them full of apartments (or rabbit-hutches as K. calls them). Hundreds and hundreds of people in those grids stretching up into the sky. Some of the windows were dark (the inhabitants abroad like us in the night), some had a simple lamp illuminating the square pane, others had the television on. It was obvious that there was a very interesting program on that evening as the blue shapes we could see sweeping back and forth across many of the windows were synchronised. All those people, living, breathing, talking in the apartment buildings straight ahead of us (along with the dwarf ghosts gesticulating and jumping around the blue screens of all those televisions), it seemed, were held within the intricate grid of that grammar book.

BACKGROUNDS

1 POLITICAL

It is 19—
X years have passed
Since the upheavals.
Everything must be placed
Against that background.

2 ÆSTHETIC

I placed a jar in Milíčov.
Unlike the nearby towerblocks it was round
And nothing much was within reach of
Its glassy empery.
I translate by profession
And have no time for trumpery:
In that age of grim oppression
It should have been the catalyst
Of change, but wasn't. It was a jar.
But then perhaps the most acute of analysts
Could have isolated the microscopic gyre
Set going somewhere on that afternoon
And Y years later stormed the parliament.

It was near the end of June,
One of those really warm evenings, the windows of the apartment
Opened wide, summer insects gliding in and out
Trafficking in small amounts of food and blood.
Thirty degrees centigrade or thereabouts.
Occasionally, the long muslin curtains lifted up and billowed.
Alex, Élisabeth and Eamon were sitting at our table.
We had just finished dinner. *L'Orfeo*
Was playing on CD (highlights, the Opera Collection label).
I went to make the coffee.
Alex was telling us about the Nixon years,
The huge complexity, the way the scandals blossomed in the public eye,
The chiaroscuro of the unknown and the known, the bright careers
Destroyed, the President believing his own lies.
From the kitchen, it seemed that Alex had constructed a maquette
Of Washington with all its shady machinations, and this
Now floated just above the table, our eyes on it,
Believable down to the last acanthus.
Each further word and phrase
Had the effect of altering it however slightly –
New colours and textures moved across its surface
As he went on explaining quietly.
Somehow Orpheus and Charon were a part of this –
The tendrils of his clauses stretching out in all directions
Kept twining themselves round the trills and dour cadenzas
Expressed into the apartment's air by Japanese electronics.
Somehow the colours of our walls were part of this as well,
The arrangement of the furniture,
The way the others sat there all the while,
The way that I, amidst the after-dinner clutter,
Was simply standing in the kitchen, thinking.
I placed the mocha on the hob and waited in the background.

UKRAINIAN CONSTRUCTION WORKERS

They travel maybe two days on a bus
        And end up here
On pittance, no insurance, bread and beer –
The paperwork looked after by their boss,

Which means that they're accounted for as goods.
        They don't exist.
If they fall off a ledge they won't be missed.
Nobody will be buried in the woods.

The street is quiet. A cloudy, wintery murk.
        At 9 a. m.
Already they've got four hard hours behind them.
They drain their beers and go back to the falsework.

Two Czechs walk by. One says, 'At least this time
        They're not in tanks.'
These days they're here to walk the scaffolding's planks
And build not blast a city in its prime –

Whichever it is is much the same to them.
        The joists, the blocks
Swung into place to found a bank or box
Five hundred lives inside (by rule of thumb),

These things are plywood-light to their strong hands.
        Their alien eyes
See straight through solid concrete to the skies
Because they know not one naïve brick stands

A chance in hell against the whim of Moscow.
                  Transparent things
Like these estates of towerblocks, civic buildings,
The new life promised everyone by Tesco,

Are what transparent men construct and tear
                  Straight down tomorrow.
What's left is less a capital and more a
Million people moving in the air.

Prague, 1996

DOGMA

after Jiří Červenka

That I am I and this world is the case,
That lamp to stool and stool to floor incline . . .
A dumb faith clamps us to the walls
While we fall aimlessly through space.

No up, no down, no right nor left.
The hand that scribbles this,
The shadow spread across this page,
Are whose?

1975

ABDUCTION

No matter how many times your neighbour greets you courteously, you never really know what's going on in his skull or his flat. Both are ciphers: the door just shut, the head just turned away, now showing god knows what expression of disgust, exhaustion, desire, or merely indifference. She could be having wild jungle parties for deaf people, he could be cutting up the bodies of young girls. Walk through this door and you'll find yourself in the middle of a fiscal crisis in Narnia, that one and King Arthur's Court is having its Connecticut session.

I had a dream last that K. was abducted by one of the neighbours to be the sacrificial victim in some occult rite and there was nothing I could do about it. The ceremony was to take place in his apartment and that's where he was holding her. The police wanted proof before they charged in, and proof was what I couldn't provide. I simply knew that she was in there and that at any moment that crazy bastard might draw a knife across her throat and I'd be standing outside in the corridor staring dumbly at his door. The police told me how sympathetic they were and that 'people come in every day with the same story and we find the corpses a week later', but then went on to explain carefully how one had to wait three months for written permission from the appropriate offices before anything could be done. I sighed and went back to staring at the door. True, he was restricting his bizarre behavioural practices to the privacy of his own apartment, but he had taken K. out the privacy of ours and into his. Such overlapping of privacies, I brooded, destroyed the whole point of the thing. My father flew in from B— to console me during my time of crisis, and the two of us stayed there waiting in the corridor, looking at the door. Occasionally, the neighbour would come out or go in to the apartment and in the short moment when the door was open, we would try to see over his shoulder, but all was blackness; nothing could be made out.

After a while the usual dream metamorphoses occurred – my father turned into Marek Strnad, the apartment building became the library of Tlön – and the crisis faded. I forgot about K.'s danger for the rest of the night, but woke up with the suspicion that our neighbour had conjured up both Strnad and the library to distract me from the horrible ceremony about to occur behind his door; and the suspicion that the meaning of his name in Z— was a combination 'magus' and 'blade'; and the suspicion that if I went to look for my Z— -English dictionary I would find that it had disappeared along with K. the evening before.

NON-ENCLAVE

this is extra ,is what's kept outside thE
door (rhymes clicking shut like locks) when it's rounD
four below and snowstorms swirl in lovelesS
-ness ,in chaos ,cancellation of uS

.whO ?that is ,of those who haunt the otheR
side of things like this page here and who rE
-side in that enclosure ,settled therE
,too cosseted to think of this no-go areA

.they're moving round inside, occasionallY
gazing out and seeing none of this ,uN
-fazed and unaware that the very grounD
where they are standing sways five floors up iN(

here are aerial shots of huge earth movements
proof of genocide or equally a
spoof of silver nitrates to turn opinion
steer attention away or towards so that it

swirls and loops back dextrously on itself
nothing sinister about it   here's some
soothing expert comment on the subject
'swirls and loops we must remember happen

. . .' but :close-up :a mind being opened by a
compact and informative piece of lead and
from it spilling outwards through the earth is
blood that brims and roils with thought careering

out beyond the enclave of the skull the
form of it whose job it was to keep the
swarming mess of waves and radiation
out   out in the swirling   looping   skies of news

)dextral chaos ,an enclave held there by thE
thinnest tissue of agreements ,vows anD
international efforts at rapprochemenT
,*lex non scripta* ,photo-ops ,translatorS

;eddying everywhere ,whose aggregate iS
whiteness ,silence ,stretching equally to thE
right and left ,a trousseau that they'll have tO
shed and pack with other worldly possessionS

AUTUMN EVENING

1   DOWN

They're home. It's evening. He's just sat down to winnow
Through human-interest stories in the papers.
She's staring.
                   – Here's one about Brazilian paupers . . .
She suddenly pounces on him and with no
Good reason bundles him skilfully out the window.
Oh, she'll go back to chopping the red peppers,
But first of all she gathers up the papers
And checks in passing if she's since become a widow.

Meanwhile the man has done his dozen cartwheels
Past floor after floor of their apartment block
And hit the deck beside the building's entry
In a difficult yoga position. Cools his heels.
His face has set hard in a look of shock
That his good wife was someone else entirely.

Entirely dead, beyond all Medicare,
He nonetheless wakes up, his clothes still sodden
With blood and guts that spilled out everywhere
On settling into his new pied-à-terre.
They spill back in again. All of a sudden
He finds himself flung upwards through the air

And being grappled into the apartment
By his good wife: she struggles with all her might
Against the monstrous pull of gravity
For him. She wins. They hug. He reads the papers
For half an hour or so, relieved and heartened
That they've pulled through, that things will be all right,
Until she tells him that the dinner's ready –
A stew of pork, adzuki, nuts and peppers.

POEM

after Ladislav Skála

I am a rock
Perched on the fifth floor
Of this apartment block

Which was exploded
About eight years ago;
That is, a breath, a cloud.

Note: In Czech the word 'skála' means rock. − JQ

63